SEX EDUCATION, VALUES AND MORALITY

Hamilton House, Mabledon Place, London WC1H 9TX

ISBN 1 85448 844 9

Typeset by Type Generation Ltd, London
Printed by KPC Ltd

Contents

Acknowledgements v

Introduction vii

Chapter 1 Setting the scene
- The context for sex education in schools 1
- Recommendations for developing a sex education programme in a pluralist society 4
  - Elements of a school sex education programme 4
  - General principles 5
  - Policy development 5
  - Classroom practice 6

Chapter 2 Getting started
- Issues in exploring faith, morality and values 7
  - Vulnerability and exposure 7
  - Power and authority 8
  - The language of values 8
  - The nature of values 9
  - Working with differences 9
  - Conflict 9
- Planning a strategy 10

Chapter 3 Workshop activities
- Name graffiti 13
- Establishing ground rules 14
- What sort of sex education did I have? 14
- The content of a sex education programme 15
- What's my culture? 16
- Groups and difference 17

Contents *(continued)*

Values continuum 19
Issues and concerns in sex education 20
Case studies 21
Case study handout 23
Sex education rights and responsibilities 25
Respect 25
Quotations handout 27
Developing a values framework 31
Action plan 32

Appendix A
Ground rules 35

Appendix B
Bill of pupils' rights 37

Appendix C
A values framework for sex education 39

Appendix D
Acknowledging differences 41

Useful resources, agencies and organisations 43

References 47

Acknowledgements

I hear and I forget
I see and I remember
I do and I understand
Traditional Chinese Proverb

We wish to thank the many people of faith and religious tradition whose thoughts, ideas, and skills provided the material for this publication: Sudarshan Abrol, Ray Appleby, Jeffery Blumenfeld, Anita Compton, Angela Flux, Jane Fraser, Sajda Khoker, Kadijah Knight, Clive Lawton, Peter McGann, Dawud Noibi, Indu Patel, Michael Reiss, Verna Richards, Gulab Singh, Surinder Saund, Rashida Sharif, Hong Tang, Diana Veasey, Margaret Vincent, Alison Webster, and Angela Wood, and those people who supported the project. Rachel Thomson of the Sex Education Forum who recorded the discussions contributed greatly to this publication by clarifying the issues, and consistently demonstrating her willingness to listen and understand. Ann-Marie Ankle typed the whole publication, and the funding body, the Health Education Authority, especially Danielle Wayne, Lorraine Hoare, Lynda Finn, and Hannah Cinamon, have helped shape this publication.

Gill Lenderyou and Mary Porter
Family Planning Association

Introduction

In April 1992, 24 people of different religious faiths and professional backgrounds took part in a four-day residential event, funded by the Health Education Authority and facilitated by the Family Planning Association. The aims were as follows.

- To clarify the range of values involved in sex education from the perspective of the major faiths practised in British communities.
- To identify a process by which people from different faiths can explore and describe their own specific values in sex education, acknowledge and understand the concerns and beliefs of others, and find ways of living and working with differences.
- To explore the values in sexual relationships and sex education that are common to different belief systems.

This resource is based on the process and outcomes of the residential event. It is aimed at education and health professionals who train and support individuals, and groups involved in developing sex education programmes in schools that acknowledge individual diversity in terms of gender, class, race, faith, sexuality, ability, and culture.

The resource is divided into three chapters.

- **Chapter 1 Setting the scene.** This outlines the legislative framework and curriculum context for sex education in schools.
- **Chapter 2 Getting started.** This describes one process involved in developing a sex education, values, and morality framework.
- **Chapter 3 Workshop activities.** This provides practical strategies for use with participants.

Appendices A – D provide some exemplary materials, which may be photocopied and used as handouts.

This publication is intended to complement the pack for teachers, *Religion, ethnicity and sex education*, which provides the personal responses to sexuality and sex education from seven different faith perspectives and one secular perspective. This resource is available from the Sex Education Forum, 8 Wakeley Street, London EC1V 7QE.

Chapter 1

Setting the scene

The context for sex education in schools

The Government's White Paper *The Health of the Nation*[1] outlined a national strategy for health in England. In relation to young people, targets have been set to reduce conceptions among the under-16s by at least 50% by the year 2000 and to reduce the incidence of gonorrhoea by at least 20% by 1995 as an indicator of HIV/AIDS trends. School-based health education, of which sex education is a component, has an important contribution to make towards reaching these targets. A comprehensive, sequential programme of school health education can be an important influence on young people's knowledge, attitudes, and behaviour. In view of the rate of unplanned pregnancy[2] and rise in the rate of HIV infection, especially through heterosexual transmission, all young people, regardless of their social, cultural, ethnic, and religious background, have a need for a comprehensive sex education programme.

The context for HIV/AIDS and sex education work in schools is changing. In July 1993, the government accepted an amendment to the Education Act 1988, which has the following effects.

- It requires governors of maintained secondary schools to ensure the provision of sex education (including education about HIV and AIDS and other sexually transmitted diseases) for all registered pupils.

- It removes the reference to HIV (AIDS), other sexually transmitted diseases, and aspects of human sexual behaviour other than biological aspects from National Curriculum science.

- It establishes a parental right to withdraw pupils from all or part of the sex education provided outside the National Curriculum in both primary and secondary schools.

In summary, sex education is now a compulsory part of the secular curriculum in secondary schools rather than a part of the National Curriculum. Parents have the right to withdraw pupils from some or all of the sex education that does not form part of the National Curriculum. School governors of secondary schools will no longer have the power to decide whether the school will provide sex education, but are required to develop and maintain a policy on the content and organisation of sex education. The situation for primary schools remains unchanged with the exception that parents will have the right to withdraw their children from some or all of those aspects of sex education that are outside the National Curriculum.

A Department for Education circular providing guidance to schools on this new framework will be issued in April 1994.

The government, its inspectorate, and the National Curriculum Council have consistently emphasised the need for sex education to be taught within a moral framework. The Education Reform Act 1988[3] requires school governors and headteachers to secure a balanced and broadly based school curriculum that promotes 'the spiritual, moral, cultural, mental, and physical development of pupils at the school and of society,' and prepares pupils 'for the opportunities, responsibilities, and experiences of adult life.'

The Education (No. 2) Act 1984[4] requires that the sex education provided should be 'given in such a manner as to encourage these pupils to have due regard to moral considerations and the value of family life.'

The importance of a moral framework as well as the importance of parental co-operation and of sensitivity to ethnic and religious backgrounds is again stressed in the HMI report *Health Education from 5–16*.[5]

Both sex education and family life education are included within the National Curriculum Council's non-statutory, but influential, publication *Curriculum Guidance 5: Health Education* (1990).[6] This guidance outlines the content and organisation for a health education curriculum across the four key stages of statutory schooling and recommends that health education should promote 'positive attitudes towards equal opportunities and life in a multicultural society by dealing sensitively with values and with cultural and religious beliefs.'

Teachers are encouraged to provide opportunities for pupils 'to assess evidence, make decisions, negotiate, listen, make and deal with relationships, solve problems, work independently and with confidence.' They are also expected to consider the 'overlapping interests of individual, group and community health' and 'the expectations of parents and other interested parties'.

Further guidance is provided in *Curriculum Guidance 8: Citizenship*,[7] which offers areas of study under the headings of a pluralist society and the family.

- **The pluralist society** is referred to as 'based on shared values and a variety of cultures and lifestyles,' which can be maintained within the framework of its laws. Specifically 'this component helps pupils to appreciate that all citizens can and must be equal. It increases awareness of and works towards resolving some of the tensions and conflicts that occur between groups that perceive each other to be socially, racially, ethnically, or culturally different. In this context it explores diversity, fairness and justice, co-operation and competition, prejudice and discrimination.'

- **The family component** acknowledges that 'pupils' experience and appreciation of family life is varied. This component encourages pupils to understand the nature of family life in all its forms and to distinguish myths and stereotypes from reality. It helps them to examine their current roles, to anticipate future roles as partners and parents, and to become more effective in their relationships.'

In April 1993, the National Curriculum Council published *Spiritual and Moral Development*,[8] which aims to demonstrate that spiritual and moral development belongs 'to every area of the curriculum and to all aspects of school life.' It highlights three areas of school life in which opportunities arise for spiritual and moral development.

- The ethos of the school.
- Across the whole curriculum (e.g. science, geography, and history).
- Collective worship.

It also recommends that schools and governing bodies clarify a set of core values to be demonstrated throughout the school.

This reflects the guidance given in the government's White Paper *Choice and Diversity, A New Framework for Schools*,[9] the precursor to the Education Act 1993,[10] which states that OFSTED will inspect and evaluate schools' provision for spiritual and moral development and pupils' response to this provision.

Such emphasis on the need for teaching sex education within a moral framework clearly raises potential issues in relation to the promotion of a specific set of morals and values, while maintaining equal respect for others.

The four-day residential revealed that there are some universal or core values, and that with careful facilitation people can work with difference to negotiate and create a values framework that is specifically relevant and appropriate to a school community. The residential participants formulated a number of recommendations for developing sex education programmes in a pluralist society.

Recommendations for developing a sex education programme in a pluralist society

Elements of a school sex education programme

Sex education is taught both informally and formally. Media messages and information to young people sometimes cause confusion over the facts and perpetuate ignorance and prejudice. Young people also learn about sexuality from the adults involved in their care and education. Such learning can be overt and deliberate, but it can also be accidental – silence and discomfort influences as much as active teaching.

School-based sex education has an important role in clarifying and contextualising mixed messages. Children and young people need sex education that encourages self awareness, self esteem, a sense of moral responsibility, and the development of social and communication skills essential for making informed decisions and maintaining personal relationships. The residential participants identified three elements in a school sex education programme.

- **Information.** Age-appropriate information on how the body works, sexuality, sexual reproduction, STDs including HIV/AIDS, and all aspects of sexual health.

- **Skills.** Communication and social skills to allow the development and maintenance of relationships, and informed choices and decisions about relationships and sexuality.

- **Attitudes, values, and beliefs.** Opportunities for young people to explore and clarify their own and other's values and attitudes and to consider how they affect behaviour. Young people can then develop a moral and values framework that is congruent with their gender, culture, race, sexuality, faith, and ability.

Active learning methods that have proved effective in all aspects of personal, social, and health education should be adopted because they can provide children with opportunities to make sense of the messages, myths, and prejudices and 'help to prepare them for the responsibilities of adult life.'[3]

General principles

Promoting any one lifestyle to young people is not good practice. Children need to develop an understanding of the diversity of lifestyles. Teachers have a responsibility to clarify their own values and attitudes so that they do not promote them inappropriately or unconsciously. They need to develop the ability to listen to the opinions, views, and beliefs of other people. Consensus is not necessary. There may be some underlying universal principles or values, but an enriching understanding can be developed through accepting and celebrating differences. Beliefs may be related to religious teaching or cultural practice, and although individuals may be unable to perceive the difference, they require equal respect.

School sex education should be implemented within a framework of equal opportunity and an ethos of honesty, trust, and respect, so that pupils can put forward and explore their ideas.

Sexuality must be seen as positive and life enriching. However although values can be taught, they are also learnt through experience and example. Values cannot be imposed, but children can be equipped with the skills needed to allow them to develop their own.

Policy development

Sex education should be taught within a values framework that has been negotiated with parents, governors, pupils, and staff. Any school's sex education policy and programme should be based on a regular assessment of pupils' sex education needs, be monitored continuously, and reviewed annually.

Teachers and governors should consult widely within communities served by the school to explore differences and deepen the understanding of sexuality and personal relationships. Each school should have a teacher who is designated to research the cultures and beliefs of the pupils in the school and to communicate their findings to staff, governors, and parents. Training for teachers and governors is essential.

Classroom practice

Sex education should be taught within clear ground rules that have been negotiated, monitored, and reviewed by pupils and their teacher.

Language must be clear and simple. Words that offend or confuse should be avoided.

Empathy can be developed by offering pupils the opportunity to explore other opinions, lifestyles, and beliefs using techniques such as stories, drama, and role play.

Sex education can be taught in mixed gender groups, but occasionally single-sex groups are appropriate in response to the perceived and expressed needs of pupils. It should be biased towards the vulnerable and hold concern for the minority.

Resources must be evaluated before use to assess their appropriateness and to eliminate elements of discrimination and prejudice such as sexism, racism, and homophobia. Pupils who make prejudiced remarks should not be attacked by the teacher: this may be experienced as threatening and result in an entrenchment of their views. It is important that any pupil feels comfortable if his or her views are challenged by the availability of new information.

Pupils should be equipped with the skills to develop a critical awareness so that they can question information, and explore their concerns and the issues that arise. Pupils should not be expected to represent their culture, faith, or any other group with requests to share their personal experience with the whole class.

Focusing on abstract principles should be avoided, but distancing techniques, where authentic life concerns and issues can be explored without exposing individuals, may be of value.

Chapter 2

Getting started

Ways in which the school community can be supported in developing sex education programmes that acknowledge the need for young people to learn to live effectively and constructively with others of different gender, class, race, faith, sexuality, ability, and culture are discussed in this chapter. Some common issues to consider before running a workshop are highlighted, and some steps for developing an appropriate local sex education, values, and morality framework are suggested. The strategy outlined is however not intended to be prescriptive. Indeed, the example cited is specific to workshop participants being recruited from the same school setting. The process itself, however, can be refined and adapted to suit a variety of training needs, in both a school- or Local Education Authority-based context. The steps to developing a framework serve merely as guidelines.

Issues in exploring faith, morality and values

The experience of exploring issues of faith and moral values in relation to sex education will probably have common features, whatever the setting – whether a two-day residential workshop for teachers, or a short session for a group of parents or governors. An awareness of the issues and potential vulnerabilities and conflicts may help those involved in this work to anticipate areas of concern and difficulty.

Vulnerability and exposure

People can feel vulnerable and exposed when asked to define their personal values. They may cope by presenting beliefs as universal statements of fact such as "everybody knows that ...." For a positive outcome, it is necessary to clarify personal values before negotiating a values and moral framework. A climate of trust has to be developed before these types of discussions can take place. Appropriate warm-up activities and ground rules are a pre-requisite for working honestly and creatively. Two ways of working with these concerns may ease the process.

- First, negotiate values from a distance by working with authentic, but not personal, scenarios.
- Second, ensure that people are not working alone, but with associates who share the same or similar beliefs and values.

Power and authority

Participants may come with a commitment to create the opportunity to discuss values and morality. However, they will have a range of different expectations, agendas, and experiences, which may make them concerned about how they may or may not 'represent' their group. It may also appear that certain individual's opinions are treated with greater authority than others, resulting in group members turning for clarification and guidance to a few participants who are perceived as having authority.

An open style of facilitation where power is genuinely shared with the participants allows them to take control of both the process and content of the workshop, to negotiate, and to have ultimate control of the outcomes. This style of facilitation can make participants and trainers feel uncertain at first and requires trust in the process and in the group. It is helped by the development of agreed boundaries, and adherence to group ground rules.

The language of values

The issues of personal exposure and power again arise in relation to language. Abstract language may lead to a situation in which people believe they are all talking about the same thing, but in reality the underlying moral and ethical dilemmas are obscured. The facilitator or teacher needs to find a balance between maintaining a ground rule that clear, plain language is used wherever possible, and accepting the use of abstract language that allows values to be explored from a distant and safe standpoint.

The nature of values

Values can be seen as either prescriptive or enabling as follows.

- Some religions and faiths offer an inherited body of wisdom and rules (divine law) where values take the form of *prescriptions* such as 'you must be married before you have sex.'
- Other moral codes describe values in more individualistic *enabling* terms as guides for personal conduct, such as 'sex is better within a committed, trusting, and mutually bonding relationship.'

Clearly the type of approach has significant implications on how values influence and inform sex education policies and programmes. Enabling values tend to facilitate consensus views, encourage discussion of different lifestyles, and can offer much to those whose lifestyle, opinions, and beliefs appear to be different.

Working with differences

Cultural values, although related to religion, may not be inherently religious. Attitudes to the philosophy and practice of equal opportunities may vary considerably along the spectrum running from a religious to a secular perspective. Most people accept the principles of equal opportunities, but a conflict with their religious principles may undermine their commitment.

The distinction between religious and cultural values needs to be explored. Understanding and awareness of these differences is developed by using a methodology of active listening centred around a respect for individual experience and belief, whatever its origin. This will help facilitate an exploration of a range of moral positions concerning sexuality, sexual health, and sex education.

Conflict

Conflict is an integral aspect of this work. It can be challenging, but is a necessary part of the process. While destructive conflict reinforces attitudes and the imposition of one view, constructive conflict leads to ways of agreeing to differ, reaching a consensus, agreeing, or compromising.

Presenting facts without offering people an opportunity to explore issues that arise may make people feel uncomfortable. Likewise, exposing personal conflicts can make people feel vulnerable. It is therefore often easier to state a value in opposition to another's opinion or belief. Identifying and exploring concerns in a way that enables people to talk about feelings safely may result in helpful discussion.

Planning a strategy

Generally, parents and teachers feel ill-equipped to explore issues of values and morality particularly in the area of sexuality and sex education. Political statements and the media spotlight on morality and family values may offer useful insights but more frequently increase the pressures and add to the confusion about the issues.

Strict religious codes on sexual matters while simplifying matters may also cause difficulties and fail to supply the practical answers people are looking for or the resolution of the dilemmas they face.

While the increasing secularisation of society provides opportunities for the development of personal moral codes the process is often perceived as unclear and the resolution of conflicts and differences somewhat daunting.

If parents, teachers, and those involved in the sex education of young people want to work within a moral framework then it is essential that they have thought about these issues for themselves.

In order to get the ball rolling, it is essential to identify an appropriate person within the school to work with. This person needs to be self-motivated with proven interpersonal communication skills and to have received appropriate training in sex education. Ideally he or she will hold a sufficiently senior position to give the work credibility.

The process in developing a framework for a school sex education programme is shown in Figure 1 (page 11), and the work of the coordinating group is summarised in Figure 2 (page 12).

Figure 1 Process in developing a framework

Step 1 Review existing policy and practice
- What is the school's existing policy on sex education?
- What is the content of the sex education programme?
- How, when, and where is it delivered?
- How are the statutory requirements going to be reviewed?

Step 2 Identify what the young people need and want
- What do the pupils want from the school's programme on sex education?
- How can the current provision be improved?

Step 3 Identify what the staff and wider school community need and want
- What do the staff and wider school community want from the school's programme on sex education?
- What skills do they need?
- What skills have they got?

↓

Step 4 Establish a coordinating group
- Who should be involved in developing the school's sex education policy and programme?
- How representative are the individuals in terms of faith, ethnicity, and social class?
- Is there a need to recruit more widely? if so, how?

Figure 2 The work of the coordinating group

Step 5 Select workshop participants
- Who should participate in the development of a values framework for sex education?
- How representative are the participants for addressing issues of marginality?
- How committed are the participants to the provision of sex education by the school?

↓

Step 6 Identify participants' needs
- What do the participants already know?
- What do the participants want to know?
- What information do participants need before the workshop?

Step 7 Organise the workshop
- What aims and objectives need to be negotiated?
- Who is going to facilitate?
- What outcomes are desired in terms of a values framework?
- What content will achieve the desired outcomes?

Step 8 Draft the framework
- What does the framework say?
- Is it a draft or a *fait accompli*?
- If it is a draft, how is feedback going to be incorporated?
- When does the framework become agreed and final?

Step 9 Disseminate the values framework
- Who is going to disseminate the framework?
- How is it going to be disseminated?
- To whom is it going to be disseminated, for example, the school's governing body, the whole school staff team?

Step 10 Monitor and evaluate the framework
- How is the framework going to be monitored?
- What is the timescale?
- What is the process for amending the framework in light of monitoring findings?

Chapter 3

Workshop activities

The following activities provide some ideas for organising work around the development of a values framework for a school sex education programme. It can be adapted to fit in with different training models, whether it is a one-day workshop or a four-day residential. All activities are designed for up to 24 participants.

Name graffiti

Aim

To introduce participants to each other and begin the exploration of assumptions, similarities, and differences.

Materials

- A large piece of flip-chart paper.
- Felt-tip pens.

Time

45–60 minutes.

Method

Participants are invited to write all their names on a large piece of flip-chart paper placed in the centre of the room and to describe in two minutes how their name relates to their own identity (i.e. culture, belief, class).

The facilitator can model this: for example, my name is Jane Mary Jones; Jane was chosen by my English mother; my father, an Irish Catholic, wanted me to have a saint's name; and my Irish grandmother married a Welshman called Jones.

After everybody has written and spoken about their name, the participants are asked to talk for about five minutes to the person next to them about how it felt to talk about themself in this way.

Processing learning (ten minutes)
- What did you learn about yourself?
- What assumptions had you already made about the other participants?
- What did you learn about the other participants?
- What differences and similarities did you notice among the group?

Establishing ground rules

Aim

To enable the group to agree and adopt a set of ground rules that will provide security for exploring and disclosing values, beliefs, and attitudes.

Materials

- Flip-chart paper.
- Felt-tip pens.

Time

30–45 minutes.

Method

If there is only a short time available a draft set of ground rules can be shown to the group and agreement sought (see Appendix A for an example).

If there is more time available, it may be more helpful for people to work in small groups and explore the manner and the context in which they want to agree to work together. These can be written on flip-chart paper and put on the wall so that agreement can be sought with the whole group. However, when ground rules are generated they need to be reviewed as appropriate.

What sort of sex education did I have?

Aim

To consider how sex education affects self esteem and prepares children for the responsibilities of adult life.

Materials

- Flip-chart paper.
- Pens.

Time

40–45 minutes.

Method

Participants work in twos or threes for 10–15 minutes and describe their own sex education, both formal and informal, and its source.

Each group of participants then records their sources of sex education on flip-chart paper. This takes ten minutes. Participants then mill around for five minutes and read each others' lists and return to their small group.

Over the next 10–15 minutes participants consider the appropriateness of their sex education and discuss the following questions.

- Was it useful and if so how?
- What was unhelpful and how was it unhelpful?
- How did gender affect their sex education?
- How did faith, culture, gender, family values, and class influence their sex education?
- How has their sex education affected their self esteem and identity?

Processing learning (five minutes)

- How could sex education help a person develop a positive sense of self esteem and identity?

The content of a sex education programme

Aim

To clarify a sex education programme for young people.

Materials

- Flip-chart paper.
- Felt-tip pens.

Time

30 minutes.

Method

In small groups participants are asked to brainstorm the main elements of a sex education programme for the pupils in their school for ten minutes. An alternative way of wording this is to ask "What are the most important things a child/young person must have learnt in terms of sex education by the time they leave this school?"

Participants then mill around for five minutes and read each others' lists and return to the plenary circle.

Over the next ten minutes the facilitator draws together a collated list and compares it with the results of a young peoples' survey or a summary of young people's needs (as described in Step 2, page 11).

Processing learning (five minutes)

- Have you paid equal attention to information, values, and skills?
- If not, what does this mean?

What's my culture?

Aim

To identify the ways in which culture affects lifestyle, attitudes, and behaviour.

Time

1–1½ hours.

Method

Participants choose a partner and work in pairs for 20–30 minutes, exploring the following questions: what is my religion? what is my class? what is my educational background? and what is my ethnic origin?

Each person has five minutes talking time while the other person listens and gives encouragement by asking appropriate questions. After five minutes the listener becomes the talker. It is important to stress that this is not a usual conversation. The listener's role is to enable the talker to explore the questions thoroughly.

Participants then spend five minutes each discussing what they have discovered about themselves while exploring these facets of culture in this way.

Still in pairs, each participant then considers the following question for ten minutes: how does my culture as discussed previously affect my sexuality and relationships?

Processing learning

The pairs join up into fours or sixes and discuss over 15–20 minutes the issues for sex education in terms of religion, class, and educational background. Questions that may help focus the discussions include the following.

- How does difference matter in the classroom?
- Should one attempt to find universality?
- What feelings do difference engender in you?
- How should difference be handled in the classroom?
- What is needed to help cope with differences in the classroom?
- How do educators keep the balance between equality of access to sex education and respect for a person's religious and cultural values?

Each group writes down a statement to describe their learning from these activities and this will be read out and drawn together in plenary.

Groups and difference

This exercise is most effective when participants have already established themselves in the group and a trusting environment has been developed.

Aim

To explore the ways people are included or excluded in groups and how this affects their self esteem.

Materials

- Flip-chart paper.
- Felt-tip pens.

Time

45 minutes – 1 hour.

Method

Participants look at each person in the group and consider silently for five minutes how each person is 'different' in some way.

The participants then brainstorm these differences for five minutes and the trainer records them on a flip-chart. A typical list might include education, class, colour of skin, culture, political persuasion, size, gender, religion, nationality, disability, age, and work.

Over the next five minutes participants are asked to place themselves into groups under one of the headings chosen by the trainer. They do this by getting up and walking around and asking questions. The activity is challenging and some people may feel uncomfortable. The trainer must move around offering support where necessary.

When the individuals have settled in groups they are asked to identify themselves, for example "we all have degrees," "we all hated school," "we were educated in religious schools." This takes about five minutes. The individuals in the small groups are then asked about how they felt joining a group: were they chosen or did they choose? can they identify the feelings? what coping strategies did they use? This also takes about five minutes.

Over the next 10–15 minutes all participants are asked to talk about the insights they have gained.

Two or three more groupings can then be tried, increasing the risk each time, but ensuring that individuals are not left exposed and vulnerable. If an individual remains excluded the facilitator can engage in conversation with them, offering support and encouragement. It is hard for those who are excluded, but making it overt can enable participants to consider how individual pupils may feel.

Ask people to get into pairs and share their personal feelings and thoughts about this activity and the effect on their self esteem.

Processing learning

Take five minutes to consider the following questions.

- What have you learnt about the effect of difference in this group?
- How does feeling excluded affect self esteem?
- What coping strategies did you use?

Take 5–15 minutes to consider how the learning from this activity can be used to ensure that all pupils are included in the classroom?

- How can all pupils be included in class, in policy making, and in programme planning?

Values continuum

Aim

To explore values and attitudes in the group and to enable participants to acknowledge similarities and differences in values relating to sexuality.

Materials

- Flip-chart paper.
- Felt-tip pens.

Time

45 minutes – 1 hour, depending on the number of statements to be explored.

Method

Participants are invited to imagine a continuum spanning the room ranging from 'I agree' to 'I disagree' for two minutes.

The facilitator then reads out a number of values statements. After each statement participants are invited to place themselves, in silence, in a position on the line that reflects their own view. The participants are then invited to turn to someone in a similar position on the line to themselves and explain why they have placed themselves there without entering into a discussion. They are asked to repeat this to someone in a very different position on the continuum. Remind participants, if necessary, that the purpose is to facilitate understanding and acceptance of difference, and that this is primarily a listening activity. Ensure that participants are not alienated or attacked by moving around the group and intervening if necessary. This should take five minutes for each person.

After a number of statements by the facilitators, participants are encouraged to suggest their own statements for exploration. Possible statements include the following.

- Marriage is essential for a healthy society.
- Homosexuality is a healthy lifestyle.
- The age for heterosexual consent protects young women and should not be changed.
- Contraception must be accessible to all men and women.
- Parents should have the right to withdraw their children from sex education.

- Couples should stay together for the sake of the children.
- If a girl under 16 is mature enough to find and attend a family planning clinic she is mature enough to make her own decisions about contraception.
- We must learn to control our sexual desires.
- Sexual knowledge encourages experimentation.
- It is not fair to have mixed faith children.
- Men and women experience their sexuality in different ways.
- It is not fair to have mixed race children.
- The purpose of sex is pleasure.
- Marriage across faiths is wrong.
- Marriage across cultures is very difficult.

Processing learning (ten minutes)

- What was the experience like?
- What difference was there between feeling your way and thinking your way to a position?
- How did it feel to expose your values to others?
- What implications does this learning have for work on values in the classroom?

Issues and concerns in sex education

Aim

To identify and consider issues and concerns in sex education, while acknowledging the whole spectrum of beliefs.

Materials

- Flip-chart paper.
- Paper.
- Felt-tip pens.
- Pens.

Time

At least one hour, depending on the size of the group and number of issues and concerns to be explored.

Method

In pairs, participants spend ten minutes identifying some of their key issues and concerns regarding sex education.

Over ten minutes in plenary the issues and concerns are then listed (e.g. marriage, homosexuality, role of women), and each group chooses to explore one topic for a further ten minutes. It is important to share all thoughts and feeling without attempting to reach a consensus. Each group is asked to record an agreed statement of one or two sentences describing the spectrum of opinion in their group. This takes a further ten minutes.

Processing learning (ten minutes)

Participants are asked to share the statements and their feelings about this activity. The following questions may act as prompt.

- What was learned about listening to opinions that differ from one's own?
- How could these statements be used?
- How did it feel to explore these issues?
- What do you think about children and young people learning about the difference and spectrum of opinion expressed today?

The agreed statements could be used as materials or guidance for developing a sex education programme.

Case studies

Aim

To increase knowledge of the breadth of opinion among group participants and enable them to practise listening to different viewpoints and values.

Materials

- Case study handout.
- Paper.
- Pens.

Time

45 minutes – 1 hour.

Method

In groups of three, participants read through the case study handout (see pages 23 and 24). Each person chooses a case study that they find the most challenging and spends ten minutes exploring the issues raised for them. The other two people help by asking open questions, such as:

- What are your fears and concerns regarding this case study?
- What do you think are the issues?
- How would you cope with this situation, as a parent, member of staff, or governor?
- What are the implications for staff and school governors?
- How could these implications affect the sex education policy?

An alternative way of carrying out this exercise is to ask each person in the trio to address these three questions.

- What do you feel when you read this case study?
- What do you think when you read this case study?
- What would you do if you were involved in this situation?

Processing learning (15–30 minutes)

In plenary participants share insights and identify some of the recurrent themes. The facilitator draws out some helpful suggestions for coping with these types of situations.

Case study handout

Case study 1

An English class at key stage 4 is studying *Romeo and Juliet*. A central theme of the play is the hostility between two social groups and an intimate relationship that develops between a young man and a young woman who belong to these groups. There are several pupils in the English class whose parents are concerned that they should only marry someone from their own social, cultural, or religious group. Some of these pupils are exploring the possibility of a free choice of partner and realise that this is creating real or potential conflicts with their parents. In many significant ways the play mirrors their experience.

Case study 2

Two boys are holding hands in a primary school playground. A member of staff overhears other children call them poofs.

Case study 3

The governing body of a primary school is reviewing a policy for sex education in response to the extension of National Curriculum Science (*Life and Living Processes*) to involve human reproduction. Some parents of 10-year-olds are concerned that their children are too young for this and believe that they alone have the right to tell their children about human reproduction within the context of their own beliefs and values and in the closeness of their own home. They have formally requested that their children be withdrawn from the sex education offered at the school.

Case study 4

A class of six-year-olds is studying the topic 'Babies.' A female member of staff has recently had a child and brings her baby into the class. The children are interested to see the baby being breast fed and having a nappy change. Several of them remark that the teacher's tummy isn't as fat as it was before and she says, "That's because my baby has been born. My baby isn't inside my tummy any more." Then one child asks "How did the baby get into your tummy?"

Case study 5

A male teacher has a year 7 tutor group and is responsible for their personal, social, and health education programme. One of the topics is menstruation. He is concerned that he might offend some of the boys and girls in his class.

Case study 6

A girl often makes suggestive remarks and behaves flirtatiously towards a male teacher who is single. Pupils are talking about it and other members of staff have noticed it. He is reluctant to talk to her privately because he fears how it may be interpreted by her and others. He also does not want to expose or humiliate her in front of other pupils.

Case study 7

Some young people are organising a disco in their youth centre. They have set the price of the tickets at £1.00 for singles and £1.50 for couples. Two young men and two young women each want a £1.50 ticket saying that they are a couple. The organisers say that a couple can only be a young man and a young woman.

Case study 8

The parents of a Muslim girl aged 15 have requested that she is withdrawn from sex education in school. She is the only person who has been excluded in school and feels very isolated. She is confused and embarrassed by some of the discussion she has overheard following the lesson. She says she cannot talk to her parents and asks her form teacher to talk to her about the content of the last sex education lesson.

Case study 9

A 16-year-old Cypriot girl who has lived in the UK for ten years is resentful that her parents rarely allow her out in the evenings. She cannot join in the social activities of her friends. She has started to get home from school later, and had told her parents that she is doing her homework in the library. One evening her father sees her in the High Street on her way home, chatting to a group of boys. He drags her home and accuses her of disgracing the family. He goes to her school where he demands to see the head of year saying he is going to send her back to Cyprus.

Sex education rights and responsibilities

Aim

To enable participants to develop awareness of young people's rights to sex education and develop strategies for achieving/delivering these.

Time

30 – 45 minutes.

Materials

Flipchart paper and pens.

Method

Divide into three small groups. Each of the groups is asked to brainstorm one of the following:

- Rights and responsibilities of young people.
- Rights and responsibilities of teachers.
- Rights and responsibilities of parents and parent governors.

Place flipcharts on the wall where all can see.

Regroup into three new groups made up of representatives of each of the original groups.

The new groups explore the following questions:

- What similarities and differences are there in the three lists?
- What themes, issues and patterns developed in your discussions?
- How do you see the relationship between rights and responsibilities in sex education?

Conclusions are fed back into the plenary group then the groups reform to consider:

- If you were to produce a charter of young people's rights what would be the six key points?
- How would you set out to introduce this into your school and what support would you need?

The three Charters of Rights and action plans are reported to the whole group.

Respect

Aim

To explore how different faiths consider the concept of respect in relation to respect for self, for others, for other people's faiths, for sexual partners.

Materials

- Quotations handout.
- Traditional to liberal continuum handout for each participant.
- Pens.

Time

45 minutes – 1 hour depending on the number of quotations (five minutes for each quotation).

Method

Individuals are asked to choose a quotation, share their interpretation of it from their own perspective, place their interpretation on the continuum model (shown on the handout), and discuss with the group the ways in which it could be interpreted across a liberal to traditional continuum.

For example the quotation offered from the Bible might be 'In Christ their is neither Jew nor Greek, slave nor freeman, male nor female. All are equal in the sight of God' (Galatians 3, Verse 28). This could imply that all people are equal and be interpreted by a liberal as totally and unconditionally accepting of homosexuality or women priests. Alternatively it could be taken literally and interpreted as referring only to gender, nationality, and equality.

It is important that people are able to identify and explore any issues which affect them personally in terms of their own development, faith, and work. The conflicts caused by apparently contradictory scriptures may undermine faith and deepen internal conflicts, but given sufficient exploration can deepen both understanding and faith.

Processing learning (ten minutes)

Participants are asked to address the following questions in pairs.

- How do you feel when you find yourself interpreting a scripture that causes conflict within yourself?, with your peers, students, and colleagues?
- What would help you deal with these feelings?
- How will the learning you have acquired by doing this exercise influence your behaviour?

This exercise could be repeated using other key value concepts such as equality in male and female relationships, commitment, and trust in relationships.

Quotations handout

Sikhism

Respect for partner

These are not husband and wife who merely sit together; they alone are husband and wife who have one soul in two bodies. (Guru Amardas Ji, Guru Granth Sahib, p 788)

O' Bride/groom make yourself up only when you have won the pleasure of your spouse. Lest he/she does not come to your bed and your make up goes in vain. (Guru Amardas Ji, Guru Granth Sahib, p 788)

Respect for others

God created light and then by Omnipotence made all; from one light has welled up whole Universe then who are we to consider who is good and who is bad. (Guru Granth Sahib, p 1349)

Say whom should I call bad or good as all the beings are thine. (Guru Granth Sahib, p 383, Guru Arjan Dev Ji)

Respect for other faiths

The methods of worship of God are countless – the religious scriptures are countless.

The devotees having different beliefs are countless.

But all this is in accordance with the will of God. (Jap Ji Sahib – Guru Nanak Dev Ji, Guru Granth Sahib, p 3)

Of all the religions, the best religion is to repeat God's name and to do pious deeds. (Guru Arjan Dev Ji, Guru Granth Sahib, p 266)

Some call you Rama, some Khuda, some serve you as Gusayan. Some call you Allah. But you are cause of causes and all bountiful. (Guru Arjan Dev Ji, Guru Granth Sahib, p 885)

Islam

Respect for self

31:18:19 And swell not thy cheek (for pride) at men nor walk in insolence through the earth for Allah loveth not any arrogant boaster.

Be moderate in thy pace, and lower thy voice; for the harshest of sounds without doubt is the bray of the ass.

Respect for others

49:13 O Mankind! We have created you from a single pair of a male and female, and have made you into nations and tribes that ye may know one another. Nor that ye may despise (each other). Verily the most honoured of you in the sight of Allah is (he who is) most righteous of you. And Allah has full knowledge and is well acquainted with all things?

24:19 Those who love (to see) scandal published or broadcast among the Believers, will have agrievous Penalty in this life and in the Hereafter: Allah knows, and ye know not.

Respect for other faiths

2:256. Let there be no compulsion in religion. Truth stands out clear from Error.

The messenger believeth in what hath been revealed to him from his Lord, as do the men of faith. Each one (of them) believeth in Allah, His angels, His books, and His messengers. "We make no distinction (they say) between one and another of his Messengers." And they say, "We hear, and we obey: (we seek) Thy forgiveness, Our Lord, and to Thee is the end of all journeys."

Respect for sexual partner

The best of you is he who is best to his wife. (Haddith)

30:21 And among His signs is this, He created for you mates from among yourselves, that you may stay in tranquility with them. And he has put love and mercy between your (hearts). Verily in that are signs for those who reflect.

4:34 Men are the protectors and maintainers of women, because Allah has given the one more (strength) than the other, and because they support them from their means. Therefore the righteous women are devoutly obedient, and guard in (the husband's) absence what Allah would have them guard.

Christianity

Respect for self

The body is a temple of the Holy Spirit. (1 Corinthians 6, Verse 19–20)

The central concept for the Christian is to love God, and to "love your neighbour as yourself."

Respect for others

Do not judge others, so that God will not judge you, for God will judge you in the same way as you judge others, and he will apply to you the same rules you apply to others, why then do you look at the speck in another person's eye and pay no attention to the log in your own. (Matthew 7, Verses 1–3)

Love the Lord your God with all your heart, with all your soul and with all your mind, that is the greatest, the first commandment. The second is like it: Love your neighbour as yourself. (Matthew 22, Verses 37–39)

Respect for other faiths

There were Jews living in Jerusalem, religious men who had come from every country in the world. When they heard this noise a large crowd gathered. They were all excited, because each one of them heard the believers speaking in his own language. (Acts 2, Verses 5–7)

Respect for sexual partner

A man leaves his father and mother and is limited to his wife, and they become one. (Genesis 2, Verse 24)

Judaism

Respect for self

O Lord guard my tongue, from speaking evil and my lips from saying untruth. (Daily Service)

Respect for others

In each person there is a spark of God. (Chassidic Teaching)

Be kind to the stranger for you yourselves were strangers in Egypt. (Torah)

Honour your father and mother in order that your days may be lengthened in the land. (Torah)

In front of the grey haired person you should get up. (Torah)

Respect for other faiths

The righteous of all nations will achieve salvation. (Rabbinic teaching)

Respect for sexual partner

If your wife is short bend down to listen to her. (Talmud)

It is desirable to make love on Sabbat of all days in the week because Sabbat is a day of joy. (Talmud)

Continuum handout

Traditional ____ Liberal

Respect for self

Traditional ____ Liberal

Respect for others

Traditional ____ Liberal

Respect for sexual partner

Traditional ____ Liberal

Respect for other faiths

Developing a values framework

Aim

To identify a range of core values that can provide a framework for the development of sex education.

Materials

- Core values framework handout.
- Flip-chart paper.
- Felt-tip pens.
- Access to a photocopier.

Time

At least one hour.

Method

Put the word 'value' on the flip-chart and ask participants to brainstorm meanings and associations for five minutes. In pairs the participants then explore their own understanding of the word 'value' for five minutes, and then in small groups brainstorm key areas that might be core values in sex education for a further five minutes.

Over the next 10–15 minutes participants circulate and read each brainstorm list and return to their small group to agree a set of values that all in the small group can accept. Suggest that it is better to have only three or four that all completely agree with than a larger number where there is dissension.

Depending on the size of the plenary the agreed values may be either fed back to the whole group for discussion, or if the group is larger, there may be another intermediate stage where the small groups join together and repeat the process of discussion, negotiation, and agreement of a set of values. This stage will take about 10–15 minutes.

When the different sets of values are finally brought to the whole group the facilitator draws them together as a final list to be discussed, negotiated, and agreed over a further 10–15 minutes.

It is probably useful if these can be typed and circulated to all participants and a time set for a final discussion before they are adopted as the agreed code of values.

Action plan

Aim

To review personal learning and to make an action plan to implement decisions made in the workshop.

Materials

- Paper.
- Pens.

Time

45 minutes – 1 hour.

Method

Participants are asked to ponder the following questions alone for 5–10 minutes.

- What are the three most important things I have learnt personally?
- What are the three least important things I have learnt professionally?

Over the next ten minutes participants are asked to share this learning in pairs, and in plenary the facilitator works with the group to summarise the decisions that have been made in the workshop. The decisions are recorded on flip-chart paper.

The decisions are shared around the group so that small groups can develop an action plan for each decision or group of decisions. The facilitator coordinates the groups by moving between them. The following questions may help the small groups to form an action plan.

- What needs to be done?
- How will it be done?
- What are the implications for pupils? for parents? for teachers? for governors?
- Who will do what?
- What support do they need?

The **SMART** action plan may be useful here: Specific, Measurable, Achievable, Realistic, Time-orientated.

In plenary the plans are then collated by the facilitator.

Closure

Allocate sufficient time (5–10 minutes) to celebrate completion of the task and to close the workshop with an activity that includes all participants. Ask participants to stand in a circle, and invite each person to share an appreciation and a farewell to the group in a way that feels personally appropriate.

Appendices

Appendix A

Ground rules

- We are working towards creating an environment of non-judgemental openness, trust, and confidentiality, which includes 'involved listening' and supporting those who experience vulnerability.
- We are working towards acknowledging diversity and celebrating difference with unconditional positive respect.
- We will actively create the opportunity to discuss values, in areas of both agreement and disagreement.
- We will clarify the status of statements, using 'I' when speaking subjectively, and be clear when speaking on behalf of a faith group.
- We will keep all personal experiences disclosed within the group confidential within the context they are given, though the points made through individual statements can be recorded.
- Groups are to be mixed in terms of gender, faith, and age, except where it is felt that separate groups are preferable.
- We are committed to fulfilling the task in hand.
- We are committed to making full use of the available time.
- We will attempt to use clear plain language.

Appendix B

Bill of pupils' rights

Developing a bill of pupils' rights provides an unequivocal and unambiguous mandate for the sex education of children and young people in school. It will reassure teachers, parents, and governors who wish to support the development of a comprehensive programme of sex education and will challenge those who argue that sex education must be limited in deference to religious views.

Pupils have a right to sex education that meets the following criteria

- Provides full, accurate, and objective information about growth and reproduction on topics including puberty, parenthood, contraception, child care, and responsible parenthood.
- Helps them to clarify their understanding about sexuality.
- Encourages core values of mutual respect, non-exploitation, and personal integrity.
- Helps them understand the importance of relationships for personal happiness in the context of their own faith and cultural values.
- Offers a supportive climate where children can disclose child abuse to trained teachers.

Pupils have the following rights

- To be consulted in the evaluation of the sex education programme and planning of a future programme so that over time the programme evolves sensitively to pupils' needs.
- To be consulted about the manner in which sex education is implemented in the classroom in connection with issues such as whether it takes place in single sex or mixed groups or which topics can be included in the programme.

Appendix C

A values framework for sex education

Teachers and those involved in sex education often express concern about which values they should model, promote, and encourage in their classrooms and schools. The following values framework presented in order of importance is an example of what a group of people of diverse cultures and faiths can develop and agree. It could be used as a starting point for teachers developing sex education policies and programmes.

Children should be taught sex education within a framework which models and encourages the following values

- A respect for self
- A respect for others
- Non-exploitation in sexual relationships
- Commitment, trust, and bonding within sexual relationships
- Mutuality in sexual relationships
- Honesty with self and others
- A development of critical self awareness for themselves and for others
- An exploration of the rights, duties, and responsibilities involved in sexual relationships
- Compassion, forgiveness, mercy, and care when people do not conform to their way of life
- An acknowledgement and understanding of diversity regarding religion, culture, and sexual orientation
- Self discipline regarding their sexuality

Appendix D

Acknowledging differences

The following agreed statements reflect the current concerns of people who have a faith and are involved in sex education.

It is probably more helpful for groups to explore and describe the broad spectrum of opinion rather than attempt to reach a consensus because each group will have their own concerns.

Teachers can use these statements as material or guidance for developing a sex education programme.

Respect and difference

Inherent in a pluralistic approach is the challenge of celebrating the differences between faiths. Respect must be given to the distinctiveness of each faith, thereby confirming each child in the belief of their faiths.

Faith and changes in society

Faiths have rules that define their practice, but need to respond constructively to the challenges they face in the changing environment, at the same time not compromising their essential beliefs and practice.

Male and female equality

All religions agree that males and females are equal spiritually in the sight of God. Within every religion there are those who believe that men and women have distinct, complementary roles. Within many religions however there are also those who believe that men and women should not necessarily occupy different roles, but should be absolutely equal in every sense.

Relationships and marriage

All relationships work with young people is valuable in helping them to be able to form stable, caring, and committed relationships. For most people this reaches its fulfilment in marriage.

Homosexuality

Homosexuality conflicts in our faiths with the traditional understanding of sexual lifestyles. For some it is completely unacceptable, while others are struggling with the tensions of wider acceptance.

Cohabitation

The increasing frequency of cohabitation outside marriage has increased dilemmas for some faiths. For some, cohabitation outside marriage devalues marriage because it does not fulfil some of the conditions required for a valid marriage. For others cohabitation is sometimes seen as a possible stage on the journey towards marriage.

Disability and sexuality

Disabled people have the right to express their sexuality within a secure environment. This raises many questions for most of our faiths that must be addressed (e.g. masturbation, contraception, marriage, procreation).

Celibacy

Different religions have differing understandings of acceptable lifestyles. For some marriage is the only possible lifestyle, for others celibacy is a positive lifestyle.

Useful resources, agencies, and organisations

A resource list for education and health professionals, *Relationships and Sexuality*, is available free of charge from the Health Education Authority's Health Promotion Information Centre (see below).

Local advice on resources and training can be obtained from the Health Promotion/Education department listed in the telephone directory under the name of the District Health Authority, and from Local Education Authority advisory or inspectorate teams.

Useful agencies and organisations

Health Education Authority
Hamilton House
Mabledon Place
London
WC1H 9TX

Health Education Board for Scotland
Health Education Centre
Woodburn House
Canaan Lane
Edinburgh
EH10 4SG

Health Promotion Wales
Ffynnon – Las
Ty Glas Avenue
Llanishen
Cardiff CF4 5DZ

The Northern Ireland Health Promotion Agency
18 Ormeau Avenue
Belfast
BT2 8HS

National organisations for the promotion and dissemination of health education messages and publications, including those dealing with HIV/AIDS and sex education.

AMANA
PO Box 2842
London W6

Black HIV/AIDS Network
BMN
London
WC1M 3XX

Brook Advisory Centres
153a East Street
London
SE17 2SD

Brook Education and Publications Unit
153a East Street
London
SE17 2SD

Catholic Aids Link
PO Box 646
London
E9 6QP

Catholic Marriage Advisory Council
Clitherow House
1 Blythe Mews
London
W14 0NW

Christian Action for Research in Education (CARE)
53 Romney Street
London SW1 3RF

Church of England Board of Education
Church House
Great Smith Street
Westminster SW1P 3NZ

Commission for Racial Equality
Elliot House
10–12 Allington Street
London
SW1E 5E1H

Council of Churches for Britain and Ireland — Youth Matters Desk
Inter-Church House
35–41 Lower Marsh
London SE1 17RL

Family Life and Marriage Education (FLAME)
Church House
Great Smith Street
London SW1P 3NZ

Family Planning Association
27–35 Mortimer Street
London
W1N 7RJ

Interfaith Network for the United Kingdom
5–7 Tavistock Place
London
WC1H 9SS

International Planned Parenthood Federation
Regent's College
Inner Circle
Regent's Park
London
NW1 4NS

Institute for the Study of Christianity and Sexuality
Oxford House
Derbyshire Street
London E2 6AQ

IQRA
24 Culross Street
London
W1

The Islamic Academy
23 Metcalf Road
Cambridge
CB4 2DB

Jewish Marriage Council
23 Ravenshurst Avenue
London
N12 0AS

League of Jewish Women
Woburn House
Upper Woburn Place
London
WC1H 0EP

Marriage and Family Project
Box 220
The Park Campus
Cheltenham
Gloucestershire
GL50 2QF

Methodist Board of Education
25 Marylebone Road
London
NW1 5JP

Multifaith Centre
Harborne Hall
Old Church Road
Harborne
Birmingham B17 08D

Muslim Educational Trust
130 Stroud Green Road
London
N4 3RZ

National Aids Trust
Room 1403
Euston Tower
286 Euston Road
London SW1 3DN

Reform Synagogues of Great Britain
The Manor House Centre for Judaism
80 East End Road
London
N3 2SY

Sex Education Forum
8 Wakeley Street
London
EC1V 7QE

Terrence Higgins Trust
52–54 Grays Inn Road
London
WC1X 8LT

World Congress of Faiths
28 Powis Gardens
London
W11 1JG

References

1 Department of Health. (1992) *The Health of the Nation: a Strategy for Health in England*. White Paper, Cm 1986. HMSO.

2 The Royal College of Obstetricians and Gynaecologists. (1991) *Report of the RCOG Working Party on Unplanned Pregnancy.* Chameleon Press Ltd, London.

3 *Education Reform Act 1988*, HMSO.

4 *Education (No.2) Act 1986*, HMSO.

5 Department of Education and Science. (1986) *Health Education from 5–16*, Curriculum Matters 6. An HMI Series, HMSO.

6 National Curriculum Council. (1990). *Curriculum Guidance 5: Health Education*. National Curriculum Council, York.

7 National Curriculum Council. (1990). *Curriculum Guidance 8: Citizenship*. National Curriculum Council, York.

8 National Curriculum Council. (1993). *Spiritual and Moral Development — A Discussion Paper.* National Curriculum Council, York.

9 Department for Education. (1992). *Choice and Diversity, A New Framework for Schools*. Cm 2021. HMSO, London.

10 *Education Act 1993*, HMSO.